GOD IN ORDINARY TIME

GOD

IN ORDINARY TIME

∞

CARMELITE REFLECTIONS

ON EVERYDAY LIFE

THE CARMELITES OF INDIANAPOLIS

Carmelites of Indianapolis

2500 Cold Spring Road

Indianapolis, Indiana 46222.2323

God in Ordinary Time

First Printing

Designed by James Sholly, Antenna

Photography by Darlene Delbecq

ISBN 1-886873-16-X

To the many people today

who are sincerely seeking to open their lives to the Spirit

through prayer.

FOREWORD

One of the first things we hear as budding Carmelites is St. Teresa of Avila's definition of prayer. "Prayer," she said, "in my opinion, is nothing else but an intimate sharing between friends."*

Each of our lives, our unique way of being and thinking, our daily encounters, conflicts, losses, observations, joys, and hopes, can become the content of this intimate sharing. The heart's longing for Unconditional Love invites us to be tuned to God's presence within and without, to be reflective about the experience of each new day, and to be alert to the deeper meaning of events and to invitations to grow spiritually.

The meditations in this book are examples of seeing life in this light and of entering into conversation with the Holy. In this relationship we can be led into an intimacy that becomes a silent being there. St. Teresa expressed it in this way: "The important thing is not to think much but to love much and so do that which best stirs you to love."**

* *The Interior Castle* IV: 1:7
** *Life* Ch. 8:5

INTRODUCTION

In a world that capitalizes on what is exciting and spectacular, it is easy to overlook the revelations of Spirit manifested in the ordinary, everyday occurrences of life. The reflections in this little book have arisen from the hearts and spirits of a religious community of women who have dedicated their lives to the practice of contemplative prayer. As will be evident throughout this thought-full collection of writings, prayer-in-depth changes the way we see things. It expands our consciousness to take in the mystery and wonder of even the most ordinary of our experiences.

The readings can be used as a springboard into prayer itself; or they can be used as a starting point for faith sharing in a community or group setting. The reflections may even be an encouragement to those who pray, to take note, by way of journaling, of their own reflections that flow from their prayer. *God in Ordinary Time: Carmelite Reflections on Everyday Life* is a helpful and practical guide for those who are seeking to strengthen the relationship between their prayer and the multiple facets of their lives.

Ginny Manss
Co-editor, *The Lay Contemplative*

When my financial records for the year finally balanced, I jumped up and danced. It was about 10:30 in the evening, and I was so energized by the joy and freedom of the event that I kept doing small jobs for hours. I was especially aware of the feeling of freedom, for I needed to have that report out of the way to be able to do another job well. I kept thinking, "I'm free, I'm free."

When I finally reflected on what I was doing, I realized that I am always free. No matter how involved, tragic, embarrassing, rushed, or important a matter at hand might be, in the last analysis I am free before God. If I do the best that I can—and even if I don't—God will continue to be God, a God who will never expect more of me than I can do or be.

In a society driven by workaholism, co-dependency, inferiority complexes, and competition, I find this experience of freedom life-giving. It speaks of the reality of our limitations and of God's blessings on them.

Our deepest source of joy and most powerful source of energy is our relationship with God, the life of God within. The passing joys and sorrows of our lives are important stepping-stones that lead us from their limited offerings to the limitless treasure that is union with God. Because they are so close to the human skin, they readily register their energy. In contrast, it takes perseverance and determination to stay with the climb of faith that keeps one going, even when the very nearness of God clouds or numbs all feeling. We can find freedom and courage in the life of faith.

Reminiscing with God

Most people enjoy reminiscing, and religious are no exception. Sometimes we get serious about it, but most of the time we retell the hilarious moments when our life really seemed out of this world. Carmelites are especially notorious for noisy recreations.

God likes to reminisce too. "I remember the days of your youth," God says in Jeremiah. At his last meal with his disciples, Jesus asked them to remember him. Reminiscing with God can be a touching form of prayer.

I still recall the time when God became more than the big picture on the wall of our kitchen. The day I heard my first story about the early martyrs was the day I learned that there really was something to die for.

Jesus and I will never forget the day I said to myself, "I am on the cross," and I thought that I would break open. We both remember how, years later, I realized that I really did break open then, and how it was the most graced moment of my life.

Reminiscing with God fills us with awe and gratitude for God's way with us in the past, and with encouragement and hope for the future. It reminds us that this faithful God always was and always will be God with us and for us.

Change

Discerned, you say—
your world, our world, is different now.
I ask,
On your new way,
whose hand is on the plow?

Dying Daily

Though martyrdom is inspiring, few of us aspire to it. While giving one's life is surely the highest expression of faith, I believe that there is much to be said about the daily manifestations of faith of the average person.

Consider the congregation at liturgy on a given Sunday. Here is a woman who comes early and enters by the side door that offers a ramp for her invalid husband's wheelchair. There is the father of four whose wife was recently diagnosed with cancer. The couple in back are mourning the death of their newborn, and the mother on the aisle is weeping for her son who has just been arrested in a drug raid.

The lives of these sisters and brothers of ours bear living witness to their faith. As St. Paul writes, they "die daily," but by turning to God in trust, they give life to our faith as surely as the martyrs have done. While we attend the liturgy to praise God, we are there also to support one another in our prayer, our presence, and our care.

I recently experienced, in a powerful way, one of life's continual opportunities for learning humility. I was in a group discussion and was struggling with the variety of ideological and theological opinions that were being expressed. I was particularly perplexed with those who seemed to want to see God only in their own way. After discussing this with a friend, I decided to take my concerns to prayer.

I knew the problem was with me, and not with those whom I was questioning. Why, I wondered in prayer, did their comments bother me so much? In the healing quiet my spirit sensed "be still and know that I am God."* Suddenly God's grace provided me with an answer. I was caught in this struggle because I wanted to rescue God, to protect God, as I deemed necessary. Laughing to myself, I realized that it wasn't really necessary for me to take care of God.

    *   Psalm 46:11

Who Am I?

"Who are we that You should even notice us?"* It is a temptation to wonder just what difference I make to God. One look at a starry sky, and it is hard to believe that my few pounds of flesh can give pleasure or displeasure to God. God is in a different league. While I was pondering this one day, a tiny, very curly-haired, very white poodle came romping into my vision, and my sense of humor, delight, surprise, and refreshing pleasure all hopped to attention. So—maybe I am God's best friend.

    *   Psalm 8

Like a Child

Little Bridget was at Mass this morning. She is sixteen months old and a delight to watch. She brings to mind the many children I once taught before I entered the monastery. Where are they now? Are they holding little Bridgets on their own laps? Or are they perhaps among the homeless or in some jail?

When I read of violent crimes, or see a homeless woman wandering the streets with her grocery cart, or hear a disoriented man mumbling near a bus stop, my mind is once again drawn to my former students. As I look at those who have met with misfortune, I try to picture them as children running happily in some schoolyard, or learning to ride a bicycle, or toddling around like Bridget. I try to hear God saying in my heart, "This is my beloved son, this is my beloved daughter in whom I am well pleased."

My Choice

I remember a Sister telling me, as a child of eight or nine, that God loves me. In my room that night I asked God, "Who are you, God? How do I know you love me?" That prayerful moment was the beginning of my conscious awareness of God and of my relationship with God.

I know that to love is to be with. I love many people and am with them all the time in my heart, the only way I can humanly be with. I am restricted by time and space. But God isn't. I remember Jesus saying, "I am with you always." God chooses to be with me.

Instead of asking God, "What can I give you, since I have nothing?" I go to prayer saying, "Here I am, God," and I give to God my time, my presence, myself. Now, I choose to be with God.

Checkout

Going through the checkout counter in the supermarket often reminds me of a line from a hymn we sang as kids: "All my sins rise up before me, all my virtues disappear." Waiting through that long line is remote preparation for judgment day. At the end of it we don't see God face to face, but we do see ourselves more clearly.

How well did I wait out the woman who was determined to find the change she needed? Did I calm down enough to even realize that I could have saved her and the rest of us some time by just giving her the change? Did I judge harshly the impatient mother of three who was doing a lot more than just shopping that afternoon? Did I become enraged at the person in the express lane with too many items? All seven capital sins seem to be on the counter waiting for me to pay up.

The weekly shopping experience might lead us into temptation, but it need not deliver us to evil. It is a call to remember that the Holy Spirit waits with us and in us, and really does deliver the daily bread we need: the bread of patience and understanding as we move along, and the bread of compassion and forgiveness when we fall short of change.

Laughter

Best friend of body, soul, and mind,
Who loses you leaves much that's good behind.
Who turns our water into wine
Save you and one who laughed and is divine.

TODAY I . . .

It has been more than fifty years since I made my first confession, but I still remember the words of one of my classmates. With utter candor, he told me that his mother had "made his list of sins" for him. (I was several years older than Jim and had labored long and seriously over my own list.) I envision a discussion beginning something like this:

JIM:

Mom, our First Communion class has to go to confession tomorrow, and I don't know what to say.

MOM:

Jim, do you remember when I asked you yesterday if you had looked in on Grandma on the way home from school? You said that you had, but you hadn't.

JIM:

Oh, yes. I did that. I lied, and that was a sin.

I heard then and remember now with envy the trust inherent in Jim's preparation for confession. This is the Eden story completely undone. No room here for Satan's great lie that makes God a jealous, damning judge. "What have I done? Yes, I did it," says this new Adam.

Freely admitting our failures to others, to God, and to ourselves may not come naturally to some, but Jim's total confidence in his mother's love and acceptance of him—sins and all—surely mirrors God's love and acceptance of us all.

BEARING LOVE'S POWER

It is usually not too difficult to overlook the faults of those I love. At the same time, there are occasions when, in the daily grind, I find myself chafing at the annoying idiosyncrasies of those nearest and dearest to me. Isn't the challenge to love my neighbor who is near merely a microcosm of the gospel's universal call to love, forgiveness, and compassion?

We all long to do something about the conflicts that devastate the world. Can this be a way for us? We are one, and the challenge for us is to realize our unity and our connectedness, to realize that everything we do affects the entire world. Our moves to understand, to forgive, and to be compassionate toward others who annoy us can mobilize to mercy a soldier who is thousands of miles away. These moves can inspire mediation among world leaders. At any moment we can pour into the world either love energy or hate energy. We can build or we can destroy. We are born of God's love, and we bear the power of that love.

AN INVITATION

We all know the routine. If the Joneses invite the Smiths to dinner, the Smiths are expected to return the favor—in kind, more or less. We do not respond to a black tie dinner with a picnic. We do understand each other's financial position, however, so the point is that we manifest a loving response with the best that we have to give.

Recently I thought of this during the liturgy of the Eucharist. Jesus has invited us to dinner. He not only offers us his very best, he offers us his very self, and he does this daily.

Our turn!

Growing in Prayer

This morning, as I made my prayer in the garden, my eyes were drawn to the path leading to the cemetery. I noticed the six trees that were planted several years ago on each side of that path. A number of the trees are sturdy; a few are dwarfs. Each of them had the same soil, the same nourishment, and the same loving care. Some of the trees let nature's gifts soak into their roots and became beautiful, while others did not flourish—seeming to reject the gifts offered them.

As I prayed, I compared the growth, or lack of growth, of the trees to my own spiritual life. God offers me nourishment every day in prayer, in reading, and in the accidents and incidents of life. Do I let them be just another exercise without meaning? Or do I let them soak into the roots of my life and let them change me?

Uncovering

I left the monastery at twilight—walking, quiet, my mind sifting through the remnants of the day. At the edge of my vision I saw her, wings fluttering in the diminishing daylight. I stopped, struck by the gentle beauty of this creature of God—orange, brown, and white etched in her wings. And then grace happened. She, uninvited, landed at my feet, wings closed, now fully camouflaged against the colors of the asphalt drive. We were there in silent dialogue—I'm not sure how long. Slowly, in my presence, she opened up, as did I. I saw her beauty, God's beauty, my beauty reflected back to me. I returned to the monastery in the darkness, light within.

In the Christian creed we say of Jesus, "he was crucified, died and was buried. He descended into hell and on the third day . . ." I suppose we have all descended into hell at one time or another. My experience of hell has been of rejection and alienation—not necessarily isolation, but times when I felt totally out of it. I've been there more than once, but God has always searched for me and brought me back on some "third day."

Because of those experiences, I know that God will never let go of me. When I descend into hell, God goes with me. Just as I can never be without the Source of my Being, so God cannot be without me—whether I "go up to the heavens or down to the nether world," as the Psalmist says. God's Spirit in the Trinity calls to God's Spirit in me and brings me back.

I am grateful for God's constancy and faithfulness, this God who holds me, descends into hell with me, and raises me up as I live out the paschal mystery of life, death, and resurrection. God, who seeks unity and oneness, can never be separated from anything that is.

The other day, on my way through the monastery toward morning coffee, I met a cricket. It was 5:15, and since neither of us was in a hopping mood, I thought, "I'll put a piece of paper down in front of the poor thing," offering to lift him gently back out to nature. By nature,

however,

being more inclined to hop than to be carried,

Jiminy took off

I took my coffee and Jiminy to prayer. They both woke me up. How often do I hop away from God's invitation to take me out of places into which I have strayed by nature? How often do I wander around unfreely just because I am afraid of God's way out?

When we are lost or feel out of place in any way throughout our lives, God is there, offering us a way out or a way through it. Once we have done our best to discern whether an offered way to freedom or growth is really of God, it is foolish to turn away out of fear. God, whose eye is on the sparrow—and on the cricket—will lift us to our true nature and beyond.

SEARCHING FOR SIGNS*

How many times have you heard the old joke about the believer who attempted to discern God's will through the practice of "Bible Roulette"? Prayerfully she took her Bible and opened it to what she hoped would be words of direction. Her first attempt landed her at Matthew 27:5, speaking of Judas' actions after the betrayal: "He went off and hanged himself." Convinced of the need for a second attempt, she closed her Bible and then opened it up again, this time to Jesus' words: "Go and do likewise." She decided to put her Bible away and to explore God's will through other means.

I remember one of my own feeble attempts. I was in Los Angeles, trying to decide whether to accept a job offer there. I asked a priest to pray over me for enlightenment and direction.

I went to bed that night still undecided about what to do. I awoke to the sound of dogs barking, car alarms ringing, and the room shaking. The Los Angeles earthquake was upon me! As I was fumbling for my glasses, the thought went through my mind: "Boy, is that priest a powerful pray-er! This is sign enough for me; I'm out of here."

I ended up staying in Los Angeles. The freeway I needed to take to my alternate destination had collapsed, and there was no other route available to me. Humorous, indeed, are God's ways.

---

* Pat Stevens, a guest of the monastery, wrote this reflection while living with the Carmelites of Indianapolis.

Hide and Seek

At times I am tempted to think that the presence of God's love was limited to the few years Jesus walked the earth. Yet I know he is risen and lives forever. And if Jesus *is* risen and people are not finding him, then somebody is hiding him—he is not hiding himself . . . He came to cast fire on the earth, and he walked Palestine as a Flame so alive with God's spirit of love that when he was blown out on the cross, the Spirit did not die. For that Fire had been caught by his disciples, who have passed it down to us through the centuries. This is the Fire of God's love for us that we must uncover and give to others, for *we* are where he is, *we* are where he lives. We carry the flame of his life, which must not be hidden under a bushel as it could not be destroyed in a tomb. That is the Presence, the meeting of Jesus that makes us more blessed than a doubting Thomas.

You're it!

Is It a Sunny Day?

When one of my nephews began to talk, he used to greet his mother in the morning with "Is it a sunny day?" That question from a sleepy-eyed toddler was surely enough to make his mother's day sunny no matter what the weather, and it also revealed that the child knew that sunny days can mean happy days. We know that too. We know what it does to a group when someone with unrestrained gloom enters a room, and we also know what a vibrant smile can do to a bus full of anxious commuters.

We all carry a bit of light and darkness within ourselves, and we have the freedom to shed one or the other on those around us. We may not be able to make peace happen in a war-torn country or to stem the tide of violence on our streets. But in our own homes, offices, or communities we have the power to let the light of gentleness and peace, and sometimes joy, shine.

STILL WATER

Recently, after the word I was needing for a crossword puzzle flashed into my mind right in the middle of a morning meditation, I began to think about the unfolding of the mystery of God that is within each of us and within every thing. Is not the quieting role of prayer the readying for that revelation?

I've heard that the best way to pray is to let the mind settle as one would a muddy pond, allowing the treasures of the stream's bed to be revealed to us. No matter the method we use to quiet the mind, at prayer we sometimes experience answers that pop up unexpectedly out of nowhere. The peaceful stance of prayer frees the mind to release what is needed for creative solutions.

But the revelation of God is not reserved solely for times of prayer. We can bring that gentle, respectful, quiet listening to our encounters with one another and every created thing. All creation speaks to us.

MONDAY MORNING

Going back to work on Monday mornings can feel like the beginning of time. We emerge from the womb of the weekend with no guarantee of what is to come. Monday mornings call for faith. What does faith have to offer at the beginning of a week? Faith is a walk into the unknown, but it is an unknown with a promise. It asks for everything, but it offers more than our minds can imagine and more than our hearts could presently sustain. It underlines our creaturehood, but it assures us of God's unconditional love. Faith's message at the beginning of the week and at all times?—Go in peace, I am with you.

As a young girl, St. Teresa of Avila* got caught up in the new wave of materialism that followed Spain's success in the Americas. She spent her free time with a few cousins who really knew how to live it up. This was not the right recipe for spiritual growth. Teresa fed her mind with romance novels and went along with the crowd until she was finally blessed with a true companion who spoke to her of God and who seriously influenced her life.

I am always a little surprised at my own inner response to reading the lives of the saints or to meeting someone who is living an exemplary life. New energy is released. Something in me seems to say that I, too, can do more with my life. It is reminiscent of the days when my piano lessons were beginning to drag and a chance concert, even on the radio, would stir my imagination about what I might be able to do with the instrument.

Excellence can magnetize and inspire us; evil and the mediocre also have their lure. Where do we find our true companions?

 * St. Teresa of Avila (1515-1582) reformed the Carmelite Order. Both mystic and a
   prolific writer, Teresa was a major influence in the life and history of 16th-century Spain.

As I read the Scriptures I hear the message of the annunciation announced to me. The Holy Spirit will come upon me, and the power of the Most High will overshadow me. I who have been barren will be filled with life-giving waters. All those I may have perceived as barren have been filled and are pregnant with the holy. We are all Christ-bearers. We carry the infant Christ, and we carry the suffering Christ as well. At times Christ is silent in me, moving the Spirit to leap in others, and sometimes Christ leaps in me as I encounter the Spirit in another.

As a community or as a family, we develop the whole Christ. In some, Christ comes to birth; in others, Christ advances in wisdom and grace. Still others are Christ suffering, or lying in a tomb. To embrace it all is to embrace the whole Christ. When Christ is in the tomb of our hearts, it is an advent time. The living waters will come and the tomb becomes a womb, waiting to burst forth into a living Christ.

IN SIGHT

When Jesus wants my attention, he says, "Let those who have ears to hear, hear." He might just as easily say, "Let those who have eyes to see, see." It is really hard to see everything that is before me with just my eyes. It is as though I wake up in the morning and say, "Today I will see as an artist. I will see the lines of trees, the skeletons of animals, the colors in the environment."

We seem to make choices. We may say, "We will see with our familiar eyes," with all of the preconceptions that implies. We may choose to see as a child, eyes wide open and curious, but not terribly informed. We may see with the wounds of past experience, or with the resurrection that was the fruit of past experience. We see with an attitude, with a mindset. "Let us put on the mind of Christ."

Pebbles in the Pool of Time

When I was a child, the atomic bomb was dropped on Hiroshima, and I rejoiced. As I remember the event today, however, I do not rejoice. The Japanese are not my enemies, and I do not understand what it means to win a war. That event is not over for me. People who are physically deformed because of that bomb still live in Hiroshima, and nuclear power is still a concept I wrestle with.

Chronological time is deceptive. It gives us the impression that an event is over and done with if it happened sometime in the past. In the present, though, when it is called to memory, the past can grow and expand.

If I still *feel* hurt or resentment, I have not grown or allowed the event to transform me. Feelings that are *remembered* rather than *felt* indicate that the past has grown in me and that I have changed. This is a moment of grace. It means that relationships can be healed even if the loved one is dead or out of contact. There is no need to live with regrets for love not given or for forgiveness withheld.

Past events are pebbles in the pool of time that continue to ripple in ever-widening circles as long as memory exists.

Transubstantiation

Like sifted wheat
we fall upon a leavened earth
that kneads us to its Center,
raising us to futures
from a consummated past.

Meeting

It was mid-morning. The sun's rays were warming the meeting room where I was about to give spiritual direction. I prayed, "Spirit, help me in my weakness. I do not know how to pray. Make intercession for me, for my yearnings that cannot be expressed in speech."* . . . I prayed, allowing these words to take root. Slowly a new attitude, a receptivity, awakened. Invitation. Allow the seeker into my God-space and wait there for God to speak. She came. We sat together, she speaking, I listening—receptive to God, to her, aware of her yearnings, my yearnings, waiting in silence until the words ripened. Were they my words or God's words? It didn't matter. What did matter is that in this sacred meeting, burden somehow lifted, faith somehow increased.

    * Romans 8:26

Spirited Matter

I cannot live a spiritual life without being engulfed by things material; I cannot be oblivious to matter. It is even possible to become mystics while occupying ourselves with material things.

I am often reminded of this as I continue to seek and find God while de-littering our grounds near the street-edge. Years ago when I first volunteered to pick up cans and bottles and candy wrappers, I began to think that my tiny actions were, in fact, a participation in our Loving God's creative movement on this earth. I feel that I am helping, in a small way, to restore God's good earth—simply by cleaning up our grounds. I pray: "Dear God, please bless those who pass this way—may the beauty of our lawn uplift them and help them to think of You, praise You, and thank You!"

TODAY I . . .

36

Holiness, like life, is a gift. Our part in both is cooperation. I suspect that people are drawn to St. Thérèse of Lisieux* because of what she did with what she had. To use the example of the glass being either half full or half empty, she chose the more positive view. She took the life that God gave her and ran with it.

If we recall the gospel parable of the talents, Thérèse's life reminds us that whatever degree of love we have received was meant to be invested and multiplied rather than buried under the unloves that are also in the package of our lives. Thérèse did not dwell on the fact that she was not perfect. She called herself a little flower and considered herself not so much a sinner as an unfinished saint.

* St. Thérèse of Lisieux (1873-1897), widely known as The Little Flower, lived a quiet and hidden life in a French Carmelite monastery. She has become one of the greatest and best-loved saints of modern times.

WHAT? NO COFFEE?

A founding member of our community died recently. After the tributes and all that funerals entail had subsided, I took some time to think about what her life had meant to me. I recalled her words about finding the nursing home a growth experience, and that she had been excited about the fact that one is never too old to be stretched. One of Sister's sayings came back to me: "Don't waste pain. Make it work for you." I began to realize the possibilities for new life that might lie in every new or painful situation.

When her sisters complained of the hardships of cloistered life, St. Teresa of Avila was quick to compare their hardships with those suffered by their sisters "in the world." Daily life is full of such calls. The smallest inconvenience that throws our routine off balance is enough to open our eyes to something new if we are willing to see it.

RETURNING

He sat, my only brother, his diminished frame sinking into the rocking chair, his energy taken by the war going on in his body. He was losing the battle; it was clear. We sat by the fire in the hearth. Ash, maple, oak, each log carrying a memory only he would know. He was suffering. It drew me into my own suffering. Why? We sat, his silence speaking of a deeper conversation. Time passed. He smiled, sending me the fire of surrender.

NOW OR NEVER

There is an integral relationship between reality and sanctity. Holiness consists simply in accepting and doing God's will from moment to moment. Such moments are gifts, sent to deepen our love for God and one another. When grounded in faith and prayer, I find that each offers us a grace, whether it is in the form of joy, suffering, peace, or dismay.

Unfortunately, many of us miss these graces. Instead, we look for heroic acts to present to God, ignoring the everyday opportunities for divine union. This is tragic, because few of us will be called to outstanding moments of faith or love. Rather, we will be called to transcend the daily occurrences of hurt feelings, unpleasant neighbors, disappointments, and minor aches and pains.

Frequently I find this call to present-day happiness challenging, because I am more inclined to focus my energies on the past or on the future. All that I can be certain of, however, is the now. Now is the time to forget, to forgive, and to heal. Now is the time to fulfill our responsibilities, to give love, and to share joy.

God's redemptive call is embedded in the immediacy of today.

Bonded in Suffering

In 1945, one month before the end of World War II, the German theologian Dietrich Bonhoeffer was hanged for his part in an attempt to overthrow the Nazi regime. During his last months in prison, he wrote that he believed that religion would change in the future, and that people would be united by the bond of suffering.

As I meditated on his body hanging between heaven and earth, as had Christ's, the words "This is my body; this is my blood" came easily to mind. His words about union through suffering followed soon after, for who is there who does not suffer?

When we find "seeing Christ in others" a special challenge, perhaps Bonhoeffer's idea can help us meet them on common ground and see them as a suffering Christ. Through them Christ also says, "This is my body; this is my blood."

Turning

The negative experiences in my life that show me how vulnerable and powerless I am can lead me to the realization of my real source of strength and courage. I believe that I come from God. I believe that God's unconditional love sustains me and that I will never be tried beyond my strength. I believe that joy is a grace that God longs to bestow upon me. In times of stress, I forget all this and begin to look to and depend upon my own resources. It is precisely when I feel weak, powerless, vulnerable, or in doubt that I must turn to God.

When we are in need, the habit of turning to God, even when we are in doubt about God, is itself an act of faith. It is an act of love that we may not feel in our hearts. It is an attempt to attune ourselves to what is, and in that attempt we touch the truth and beauty and goodness that is God.

Hidden Friends

I like to pray in the early morning when all is quiet. In the summer, I frequently go outside and walk on the monastery grounds or sit in our courtyard. In the winter, when the mornings are dark, I prefer to sit in my very small room. The windows are high, so that only the sky and the tops of trees can be seen. Periodically, the twinkling red and white lights of a plane far up in the heavens punctuate the blackness.

I try to picture the passengers traveling to their destinations, and I wrap them in prayer. Where did they begin their journeys? What loved ones wished them well? Whom will they meet when they land? What calls them to be traveling at this hour? I hold them all in my heart and pray for their safety and their happiness, though they do not know this unknown friend sitting in a monastic cell. Sometimes I wonder if one of them is looking down on the miniature trees and houses, seeing the lights of the city, sending down silent blessings upon me—an unknown friend cradling me in prayer. We could be sending arcs of blessing like rainbows through the skies.

All who are free

tell me a thousand graceful things of you;

all wound me more and leave me dying

of, ah, I-don't-know-what behind their stammering.*

John of the Cross**

The shepherds of the galaxies, the Hubble Telescope astronomers, have released photos of the universe from fourteen billion years ago. As I attempt to fathom the very notion of billions of years ago, my gaze settles on a large maple tree in the cloister. Nestled in the fork of the trunk and a snow-covered limb, a squirrel wrapped in its tail is sleeping. Its ability to slumber while balanced so precariously is as mind-boggling to me as the distance of light-years—equally deserving of the I-don't-know-what of God.

42

  * Source: John of the Cross, "The Spiritual Canticle," in *The Collected Works of St. John of the Cross*, trans. Kieran Kavanaugh, OCD, and ed. Otilio Rodriguez, OCL (Washington, D.C.: ICS Publications, 1991), The Poem, Stanza 7, p. 472.

** St. John of the Cross (1545-1591) worked with St. Teresa of Avila to reform the Carmelite Order. His poetry is among the masterpieces of Spanish literature.

When I lose all sensory awareness of the presence of God, and my prayer consists in wandering around in my mind wondering where Jesus is; when my feelings are bone-dry; when the only encounters I have are interruptions from strangers (or friends); and when all I have at the end of prayer is the realization that it is time to go back to work—I call this a Mary of Magdala moment.

On the first Easter, when Mary of Magdala went looking for Jesus, she thought she knew where he was. She had held his dead body and had laid it in a tomb as recently as Friday. But this Sunday morning things had changed. He was not there, and she was beside herself with grief and loss. When Jesus finally appeared to her, she was unable to *see* that he was the stranger before her. She was not permitted to touch him. His words to her were simply "Mary" and "Go." And he gave her a job to do. Mary left her time of search rejoicing in the knowledge that Jesus still lived and was with her.

When we seek Jesus in prayer, he is there, even when we don't know it. If we can see Jesus in those who interrupt us and hear his voice when others call, if we can remember that it is Jesus who calls us by name to prayer in the first place, then we, too, can leave our time of seeking God rejoicing in the knowledge that Jesus lives and remains with us. Mary didn't find him; he found her.

Pictures on a wall or desk, billboards we see on the way to work, occurrences such as the chiming of a clock or getting caught in traffic—all of these can become reminders to us of the presence of God. It is the mystery that enables us to pray always and everywhere.

I cannot be aware of the Divine Presence continuously, but my heart can be dedicated to God at work or at play, as well as at times especially given to prayer. In these latter times of solitary quiet prayer, I can make the conscious acceptance of all that I am in God and say "yes" to what life has in store for me. This conscious commitment is the core that unites all that I am and all that I do into one timeless gift to God. Then whatever I am doing, I carry the assurance that I am in the Lord. This is the mystery of the abiding presence of the Holy Spirit within each of us. This is the Spirit that prays in us when we do not know how to pray.

46

GOD WITH US

Jesus promised to be with us until the end of time. That is both reassuring and challenging, for the word "us" can be a real snag. When your day is disturbed by someone who seems to be constantly at your heels, you may tell yourself, "If I could be that present to God all day, I would be a saint." Yet you soon realize that, aha, you have been that present to God *in* that person all day. Now what? Guilt, if you were obnoxious? Useless. Pride, if you were kind? Just as useless. Awareness? Yes. God is with us that we may be with God.

I Can't Pray

Imperceptibly over time a kind of numbness began to affect my mother's extremities—extreme polyneuropathy, the doctor called it. She lost the use of her hands and feet, and she was confined to the easy chair she once used to relax in. It was her home by day and her bed by night. No longer could her hands hold pots or pans or her fingers ply the crocheting hook.

The loss of sensation was not the first loss. She had lost a child, a mother, a husband. Death had claimed most of the friends and neighbors with whom she had enjoyed phone visits. She would say in one breath, "I can't pray anymore," meaning she could not pray as she once had, and in another, "Pray? That's all I can do." I think my mother achieved a prayer of union—God was her only reality. She never sat in a monastic cell to make her hours of prayer; nor did she meditate by a river. What she did was accept the joys and sorrows of her life and surrender to them both—as gifts from God. She lived the paschal mystery with its daily dyings and risings, and in the end, she no longer prayed. She *was* prayer.

Seeing from Afar

When St. Thérèse found herself struggling with a difference of opinion with her sisters in the monastery, she sometimes imagined herself in another community evaluating the conflict from afar. Seeing it all from a new perspective, she was able to smile at the over-importance that she had placed upon it up close.

How often I leave an incident and, after thinking about it, wish I could do it all over again. If, however, as I experience the situation I imagine myself an onlooker, I find that while I am at once totally present to all involved, I can simultaneously monitor my actions without the pull of emotions that could limit my freedom. I am there—with the advantage of seeing from afar.

Empathy

Whenever I think of Edith Stein,* I marvel at her ability to reach out to others with the limitless love of God. God, who in Christ sees the Christ-life in all, sees every person as child, anointed and beloved. Edith developed the quiet art of listening to the Holy Spirit within, and this enabled her to begin to see as God sees. She believed that the Spirit is alive in each one of us, waiting like a tender bud, ready to open and reveal itself at the least breath of interest and willingness on our part.

Quiet listening to the whisperings of the truth within can lead us to a spirit of solidarity with the neighbor in need, calling us to creative collaboration for the good of all. As we reach for Edith Stein's degree of perception, perhaps the neighbor whom we must first welcome is the Spirit of God within us.

---

* Edith Stein was a Carmelite nun who was killed in the gas chamber at Auschwitz. She is known for her work in phenomenology on the subject of empathy.

FINDING OUR GOD-SPOT

Do you remember the story of Achilles' heel? It seems to me that it is *our* story—the story of the human condition. My favorite detail is how Achilles' mother, the sea-nymph Thetis, dipped him into the river Styx to make him immortal. Wherever the water touched him, Achilles became invulnerable. But the place where Thetis had hold of him, his heel, the water did not touch.

We come into the world very vulnerable; as we grow older and develop our defenses, we learn how to protect ourselves from others and become somewhat invulnerable. But in God's goodness, we are each given a "God-spot," a place where we are particularly weak, a place of vulnerability. I call it my original sin, but it is also the place where God has access to my heart. When I am feeling completely together or on top of things, some incident comes along and hits me in my "God-spot," forcing me to acknowledge my weakness. It keeps me in touch with the human condition, my dependence on God. We need this weakness, this Achilles' heel, the place where God holds us, has access to our heart, connecting us to the One who loved us enough to make us vulnerable.

VISITING DAY

A potted plant and candy box,
the soft and gentle caring talk,
the slow, short walk that does not take me home.

THE GIFT OF EVERYTHING

My niece Maureen was a beautiful young woman of twenty-nine. She had so much going for her: a happy marriage, a precious little baby boy, and a computer position at UPS that challenged her in every way. She loved life.

Suddenly she was diagnosed with osteosarcoma of the jaw, a rare type of cancer. The news was a shock, but from the outset she worked toward acceptance. Her concerns were for others: her husband, baby, family, friends and co-workers, and all those who cared for her. Then the real bombshell came—brain cancer. Surgery and radiation did help for a period of time, but after some months, the doctors told her that nothing more could be done.

At times the going was rough, but, like Job, Maureen chose to trust in God. She said to me, "God is always there for me. The short time given me has been filled with happiness—a loving husband, the joy of motherhood, wonderful friends and co-workers who have followed me through this journey to new life."

Maureen's example sheds light on what holiness really is in this life. She teaches us to open ourselves to God through her gracious acceptance of the loss of all that was given to her.

GRIEF

Grief is the dessert of a full life.
Napkin to eyes,
we leave the empty table of what was,
our hearts heavy with gratitude inside-out.

COMPLETING THE PUZZLE

Recently I found myself stumped on an entire corner of a crossword puzzle. I had confidently filled in RANCHTYPE where it asked for "Like some houses," delighted to have come up with such a long word. I was sure of the first letter, and the word fit perfectly, but nothing around it seemed to connect.

A word that looked like it belonged in the block kept teasing me to try it, but it conflicted with RANCHTYPE, to which I was becoming more and more attached. Finally I reluctantly erased RANCHTYPE and wrote IN TIME where the puzzle asked for "Eventually." Suddenly word after strange word popped out at me, and within about thirty seconds the entire corner of the puzzle came together.

Often we go to God with a favorite word written in the stone of our willfulness. When we are willing to let God erase our plans and agendas—to let willingness replace willfulness—we come away from prayer with a new idea, God's word, and we are more together with God and ourselves than before we began.

PRAYING SCRABBLE

The last two times I played Scrabble I was left with a Q—worth ten points—when every U was tied up on the board. There was no way to get rid of that very valuable block. That's what I call a lose-bad situation. At such times I am reminded of: "If you lose your life you will find it; if you gain your life you will lose it." Card games in which you win by putting down all of your cards can teach the same lesson. Talents, money, personality, beauty—all of these are aces in your hand, to be recognized and dealt with for the good of the game of life. To win, however, one must give it all away and end with empty hands. I need to pray Scrabble or cards more often.

TODAY I . . .

52

53

Doing Without

During World War II, just about everything we purchased in my town was either hard to find or rationed. Patriotism was high and few complained, because we all knew that our sisters and brothers in the armed services were doing without. We wanted to be one with them in the war effort. Scarce items that were acquired honestly were neither flaunted nor hoarded, and those who got what they wanted through the black market were considered traitors of sorts. We knew there was a war going on.

Today we speak of a war on poverty, on drugs, or on crime. In some way the causes of all the underprivileged—minority groups, women, children, the disabled, all who are less than free to live fully human lives—also call for a declaration of war against the evils that enslave. Do we have enough Christian patriotism to join our sisters and brothers who are doing without?

Keeping an Eye on God

One of my favorite hymns reads, "O God, you are the center of my life." Some days I wonder about that. In an attempt to live consciously, it is easy to go overboard and get bogged down in examining my life rather than living it. St. Teresa of Avila's sisters must have had that problem, because she wrote to them: "All of our troubles come from looking at ourselves rather than the Lord." In the journey of life, when we look at ourselves in the rear-view mirror instead of looking at the road, the Way, we can run over people and lose our direction. Focusing on the Way creates the shortest distance between two points, now and eternity.

SCRATCH MY BACK

One of my favorite outings is a trip to the zoo. There is so much to learn from observing the different animals. There are signs that alert the viewer to specific behaviors to watch for at particular exhibits. When you visit the baboons, you see a sign reading: "You scratch my back and I'll scratch yours." Baboons do a lot of that!

Reciprocity is something I can understand. I have expectations, such as: I sent them a Christmas card, so they should send me one; or, I asked them to dinner, so they should invite me. But this is not a Christian virtue. According to the gospel, I am called to love my enemies and to do good to those who persecute me. To be a Christian means at times accepting the challenge of detaching myself from my human expectations.

Among my fondest desires are to be accepted, understood, and loved, to live in a life-giving environment, and to have my talents recognized and used. These desires are not wrong, but if I am not detached from them, I will never find peace of heart.

Love, appreciation, and acceptance are not of themselves reciprocal. They depend on the other over whom we have no control. We may scratch someone's back, but that does not mean that she or he will scratch ours. God does not wait on our worthiness to lavish love and forgiveness upon us, and we who are made in God's image are called to a non-reciprocal love, a non-reciprocal forgiveness, a non-reciprocal acceptance. To be followers of Christ is to choose to scratch unconditionally!

When his first son was about a year old, my brother, only half-jokingly, said of him, "The kid makes me nervous. He goes around acting as though he knows something I don't know." There is something about the freedom and trust of a loved child that speaks of the beyond. Children live an unabashed "I am" that ignites a spark of wonder, if not envy, in the socialized adult. It is as though they have been in touch with the initial act of creation so recently that the veil between the divine and the human has not completely fallen into place.

Prayer, opening oneself to God, can thin the veil of the mystery of the Creator. A child-like approach to nature, to one another and to life, and a single-hearted search for and openness to God can ready us to experience breakthroughs of the Divine in everything, in each event of our day-to-day lives.

Artists wait for hours for the right sunset or sunrise. Writers wait for the words to rise to their fingers. Pray-ers watch and wait for the revelation of God that is always a mystery to their minds, but which they somehow recognize with their hearts. Children tell us much before they can talk. Prayer can thin the veil of the mystery of the Creator. God speaks without words.

FOUNDATIONS

Some of the work that I do involves coordinating the maintenance of the monastery building, so I am very aware of the importance of a solid foundation. When I attend a meeting at another monastery, I find myself noticing how the brick and mortar is holding up there. Jesus tells us that our lives also need a solid foundation, and he tells us to take care lest we build on sand. His bedrock for eternal life is "wholehearted love for God and love for neighbor as oneself." For centuries people have striven to build their lives on charity, and I believe that each of us has a way of living out our love that tells something about who we are. St. Francis wanted to be "an instrument of [God's] peace." Blessed Elizabeth of the Trinity, a ninetenth-century French Carmelite, called herself a "house of God." I suggest that for each of us to discover *our* way—little or big—and to name it, if only to ourselves, would be to give ourselves a point of reference, an identity, that would strengthen and energize our relationship with God and with others.

NO DEAD ENDS

As I grow older and more sensitive to my own part in the social sins of the world, and as I read the challenges that Jesus offers us in the gospel, I become more and more aware of the cost of discipleship. The gospel continues to be good news, however, for we know how Jesus responded to the weaknesses of others. Through his resurrection he took the past of the apostles and forgave the worst of it and saved the best of it. He conquered the future by making even death a door to be opened instead of a dead end. Most happily of all, he gave each of us his Presence, his Spirit, to be the way through which we live toward that future which "eye hath not seen nor ear heard." No matter what our life situation is at this moment, no matter where the world seems to be going, this is the Jesus of our faith who continues to be our hope.

Midnight Moments

While visiting a hospital, I had the privilege of witnessing a father seeing his newborn baby for the first time. He was speechless, but his eyes were aglow as he looked at the baby swaddled in bubble wrap.

When Jesus was born in the stable and placed in a manger, I don't think Mary or Joseph thought about anything but the joy of having and holding the child. At that blessed midnight moment, the future did not exist: the rejection, the betrayal, the misunderstanding, the violence of scourging and crucifixion. There was only joy and gratitude. What was to come could not impinge on what was present. We all need times like that—midnight moments—when the wonder of the present fills our being, and the past and the future cease to exist.

Untangling

The house is empty now. All of us have moved away. Today, it seems clear. We were born too closely together.

Again we are in conflict. She speaks with words that cut. I wince. No, not again. I clench the receiver, my stomach tightening into a familiar knot. She, my sister, mystery. She says, "I don't have that need." But I know I do. There is a long pause. I see her alone in her bedroom. My breathing slows and my shoulders soften. More words are spoken. Another pause. I see her when she was ten, sitting on our front stoop stroking our cat. I breathe in her loneliness and let it fill me. I soften some more, edging myself into her truth. When we were young, we would stay up late at night sharing our dreams. In my heart, I send her one of her old dreams, and leave it to do its work.

Matthew tells us that Jesus, after his baptism, was led by the Spirit into the desert in order to be tempted. I've often wondered about that. We have just been told that he was the "beloved Son in whom God was well pleased." Why did he need to be tempted? He was a young man of thirty years, full of zeal. Did he need to face his own helplessness, his own creatureliness, his own vulnerability?

I sometimes think of him there roaming about for forty days with little or nothing to eat or drink. As time wore on, I imagine he looked a bit wild, his hair dirty, his clothes tattered. Did he look like the outcasts, the lepers, the unclean, the tormented women and men who roamed the desert with him—those who were not allowed to be with the acceptable people of his society? Did he see their tortured eyes, their hopelessness, possibly their ministry to one another? And when he had reached his limit of endurance, could not the angels who ministered to him have been those very outcasts, or perhaps some Samaritans passing along the way? Maybe it was this experience that gave Jesus a new understanding of his mission: to give sight to the blind, to heal the sick, to free the oppressed.

When I experience my own desert-times—times of alienation, barrenness, or aloneness—perhaps I have been led there by the Spirit to face my own demons, to let them emerge and rise before me, and to learn my own powerlessness and weakness, to enable me to see my oneness with others who feel alienated, rejected, barren, alone. I need to recognize and acknowledge those whom I have kept at a distance as those who can broaden my vision, who can stretch my boundaries and free me from the trap of judging who or what is acceptable. Our demons can minister to us if we acknowledge them, and those others whom we hold at a distance may well be the angels who will bring us to wholeness.

THE END OF VIOLENCE

Violence is a contagious dis-ease that infiltrates the lives of all those who come in contact with it. It is a rare person who does not experience the symptoms of anger, hate, or revenge. The victim or witness is breathing the contaminated air of a foreign atmosphere.

Violence generates an energy that urges action, and it is vital to realize that we have the freedom to choose how to use that energy. To return to the stability of our true self, to return to our formerly healthy space, we must flush violence out of the system.

We all have within us a survival back-up of spiritual gifts of charity, joy, peace, patience, mildness, and more—the healing white cells of the soul. This inner power can be released, despite the anger, tension, and horror we may feel.

By deliberately choosing to pray for the offender, by reaching out to others in acts of goodness that engage our thoughts and change them to thoughts of love and peace, we clear the air of violence and turn in the direction of healing and well-being.

Every time we respond with love and forgiveness, all humankind is raised up to a new vision and quality of life. This is salvation. This is mirroring the God who makes good come of evil. This is the beginning of the end of violence.

BEYOND DEATH

O Death,
Where is your sting—
You who bring the breathless beauty
of autumn and of spring?

What Is Wanting

Some days I think that God has a need for gratitude. It keeps welling up inside me, and I find myself praying prayers of thankfulness concerning just about everything. It is as though it is being pulled out of me. This is really not such a strange occurrence. If we believe that suffering is redemptive, and that what some people suffer is for the salvation of others—"filling up what is wanting in the suffering of Christ"—then it is not so odd to suppose that there is a measure of gratitude asked of us that Jesus did not fulfill in one lifetime.

The prayer of thanksgiving can also be a lifesaver when we feel empty at prayer times, when our hearts are dry and we seem to be wasting our time. When this state continues, along with being grateful for what we experience as blessings, we can thank God for the emptiness, and just give God the time. We are never left with empty hands before God.

God's Way

It is possible to try so hard to do God's will and God's work that we get in God's way. Each of us is still in the making, but as responsible for our lives as we are, we do not have to do it all alone. God is creating the world through us, but we are part of the world that God is helping us to create. If at times we can just be, just quietly sit in the sun of God's love for us, if we can believe that the One who formed us in the first place is waiting to transform us in the embrace of love, then God will increase and we will decrease, in the best sense of the word, in what we are doing with our lives.

TODAY I . . .

64

ACKNOWLEDGMENTS

There are a number of friends who have been particularly helpful in reviewing the reflections and giving us valuable suggestions. We wish to thank Rosie Borman, Clare Bosler, Kathy Brinkman, Bill Carr, Max Case, Judith Cebula, Cindi Fankhauser, Mary Ann Grogan, Marcia Hadley, Joyce Janca, Lou Ann Lanagan, Ginny Manss, Connie Marquis, Kevin McKinney, Andrea Neal, Elaine Theisen, John Thomas, Miriam Tjader, and Shirley Wishoski.

We give special thanks to Darlene Delbecq for the gift of her photography, to Kathleen Norris for her kind words, to the estate of May Sarton for the use of her poem, and to Ginny Manss for the Introduction.

In addition, we extend our gratitude to George Menke, SJ, for his editorial work, to Linda Hegeman for her encouragement, and to Mary Jo Weaver for the title and her direction.

Joanne Dewald, Prioress

Nancy Bishop

Teresa M. Boersig

Ruth Ann Boyle

Martha-Marie Campbell

Rosemary Crump

Jean Marie Hessburg

Rita Howard

Anna Mary Larkin

Marcia Malone

Jean Alice McGoff

Elizabeth Meluch

Mary Rogers

Rachel Salute

Helen Wang

In spirit we travel

the road to transformation,

and we are nourished and guided all the way.

Created by God who is For us,

companioned by Christ who is With us,

and led by the Holy Spirit who is In us,

we come to a wholeness

that partakes of the holiness of God.

Glory to You, Source of all being,

Eternal Word, and Holy Spirit,

as it was in the beginning,

is now, and will be forever.